ADVENTURE SPORTS

MOUNTAIN BIKING

ADVENTURE SPORTS

MOUNTAIN BIKING

SCOTT WURDINGER & LESLIE RAPPARLIE

CREATIVE EDUCATION

Published by Creative Education
123 South Broad Street, Mankato, Minnesota 56001
Creative Education is an imprint of the The Creative
Company

Design and production by Blue Design
(www.bluedes.com)
Art direction by Rita Marshall

Photographs by Alamy (Buzz Pictures, Michael Clark,
Gary Crabbe, Mark A. Johnson, J Marshall – Tribaleye
Images, Photo Central, POPPERFOTO, Powerhouse
Digital Photography, Ltd., Seb Rogers, Tobin Rogers,
SHOTFILE, doug steley, Stock Connection Blue,
Stock Connection Distribution, David Wall, Tom
Way, Westend61), Vertical Perceptions
Photographs on pages 11, 14, 15, 16-17 copyright Kirk
Novotny, VisionaryEnchantment.com

Printed in the United States of America

Library of Congress Cataloging-in-Publication Data

Wurdinger, Scott D.
Mountain biking / by Scott Wurdinger and Leslie
Rapparlie.
p. cm. – (Adventure sports)
Includes bibliographical references and index.
ISBN-13 : 978-1-58341-396-8
1. All terrain cycling—Juvenile literature. I. Wurdinger,
Scott D. II. Adventure sports (Mankato, Minn.)

GV1056.W87 2006
796.63—dc22 2005051784

First edition

9 8 7 6 5 4 3 2 1

MOUNTAIN BIKING

A rocky trail lined with hairpin turns winds up a forested mountain. Two bikers push hard, standing on their pedals as they strain to climb the trail's sharp incline. Their bodies tense as they lean forward, trying to gain momentum and speed. Sweat drips from under their helmets and down their cheeks, and all of their concentration is focused on keeping their bikes moving to the top. Occasionally, they breathlessly cheer one another on, making sure that no matter how tough the ride, they will both reach the summit.

Once the bikers make it to the top, they give each other a high-five and stop to catch their breath as they look out over the amazing view before them—a wide expanse of wilderness stretching beyond the treetops into endless space. After a few moments, the bikers smile and point their bikes back down the trail. With one last look around, they push off, gaining speed

Mountain biking is a combination of speed, sweat, and often breathtaking scenery in the great outdoors. It is also a sport that embraces a real element of risk, as many bikers traverse steep hills, sharp corners, and daunting rocks.

as they bump over ruts and mounds, sometimes even flying in the air for brief moments. Their eyes get big, and their breath comes quickly as they execute dramatic turns and squeeze through tight spaces. Too soon, the ride is over, and the bikers rest at the bottom of the trail, already dreaming of their next trip to the top.

Ned Overend, winner of the first cross-country World Mountain Biking Championships in 1990, describes the essence of mountain biking: "It's a feeling you get on certain trails, when you're reacting like you and your machine are just one thing. It's the feel of physical exertion and speed and technique all wrapped into one." Mountain bikers around the world know this feeling. For some, it comes from careening downhill; for others it can be found in a strenuous uphill workout; still others find it on a quiet back-country trail—but for all mountain bikers, the biggest thrill comes from just being on their bike.

The allure of mountain biking varies from rider to rider. Some are drawn to the exhilaration of speeding down rugged hillsides or the workout of climbing up them, while others appreciate the quiet moments to be had exploring backcountry trails.

The Birth of The Mountain Bike

Before bicycles were invented, people had limited or expensive means of transportation. Walking was a slow but ever-present option. Horses and carriages were expensive, high-maintenance alternatives. The invention of the bicycle revolutionized the world of transportation, enabling people of all ages and classes to move about quickly and easily. Today, people across the globe own bicycles and use them for a variety of reasons, from getting to work and running errands to exercising and enjoying the outdoors.

The original idea for the bicycle came from Leonardo da Vinci in 1490. Although da Vinci's blueprints were far ahead of his time, the model he drew is thought never to have left the drawing board. Most historians believe that primitive forms of the bicycle were developed in the 1790s, but bikes that resemble the modern version, with cranks and pedals, have only been around since the 1860s. The first modern bikes looked much different than today's models, however, with a large front wheel and heavy iron tires. In the 1870s, James Starley changed the face of bicycling when he created rubber tires, making the ride over bumpy cobblestone streets smoother and more enjoyable. Over the next several decades, bicycle technology continued to advance, with the addition of spring-seats, adjustable handlebars, wheels of equal size, and other improvements.

Modern mountain bikes feature only the same basic framework as bicycles of the early 1900s (opposite). With their light frames, knobby tires, and sophisticated shocks, mountain bikes are a far different breed than the road cruisers of decades past.

Mountain bike pioneers such as Gary Fischer (above, center) began their bike racing careers on the rolling mountains of Marin County, California (opposite). Today, tourists visit the area to experience the scenic trails and grueling racecourses that inspired the sport of mountain biking.

Compared to the long history of the bicycle, the concept of mountain biking is very new. In the early 1970s, three Californians, Otis Guy, Marc Vendetti, and Joe Breeze, rode their one-speed, **balloon-tire bikes** up the trails of Mount Tamalpais, a 2,571-foot (784 m) peak in northwestern California. Although the bikes' single gears made pedaling uphill nearly impossible, the men pushed to the top again and again for one reason: to experience the thrilling ride downhill.

In 1974, at a **cyclo-cross** race in California, Guy and Breeze, along with friends Gary Fischer and Charlie Kelly, took notice of bikers sporting balloon-tire bikes with thumbshift-operated **derailleurs** and **drum brakes**. After seeing these bikes, the four men developed their own version of the balloon-tire bike with similarly sophisticated **components** to enhance performance and ease of riding on inclines. By October 1977, Breeze had completed a model of the first-ever mountain bike. He called his bike—with its fat, knobby tires, lightweight tubing, and sophisticated front and rear derailleurs—the "Breezer." Building ten of these bikes, Breeze opened the way for the sport of mountain biking to become a worldwide craze.

The Right Gear for The Adventure: The Bike

Today's mountain bikes have come a long way from the Breezers of the 1970s. With a wide range of choices in frames, suspension systems, saddles (or seats), brakes, and more, mountain bikers today can customize their rides to fit their personal preferences. From the fancy and fully outfitted to the minimalistic and simple, today's bikes can satisfy all tastes and needs.

The frame is the backbone of every bike, providing stability and form. Originally, most bike frames were made of steel, but many bike manufacturers today are moving away from this material. Although steel frames are strong and springy, they are also heavy, making steel bikes cumbersome. While lightweight steel is used for some bike frames, it must be welded by highly skilled workers, making the process expensive.

Today, most mass-produced bike frames are built from aluminum alloy. These frames, although strong, lightweight, and rust-resistant, are stiff and unforgiving. Vibrations caused by a bump or rut in the trail are transferred directly to the biker's body instead of absorbed through the frame. In addition, aluminum frames usually do not last as long as steel frames. They are, however, relatively cheap, beginning at about $150, making them ideal for recreational mountain bikers who enjoy the sport but don't want to spend a lot of money.

Professional riders, whose bikes and bodies regularly endure the punishment of riding on rough trails, on the other hand, want the best materials available for their bikes. Today, most of the bikes ridden by mountain bike professionals are made of carbon fiber composite, a combination of carbon fibers and **epoxy resin**. Carbon fiber frames require numerous hours of labor to build, since the material must be layered. As a result, these bikes are fairly expensive, costing anywhere from $1,000 to $3,000 or more. In addition, while carbon fiber composite absorbs vibrations well and is extremely lightweight, it can be fragile and, like alloy, may fatigue quickly.

No matter what their frame is made of, all mountain bikes come in two different styles: hard tail or soft tail. The bikes take their names from their suspension systems. A hard tail bike has a front suspension but no rear suspension. The front suspension consists of shock absorbers located at the **front fork** of the frame of the bike. The back half of the hard tail bike has a solid frame, leaving the biker's body to take the brunt of the shock. The soft tail bike, on the other hand, sports both a front and rear suspension. The rear suspension, which is located on the backside of the bike, causes the bike seat

The front and rear suspension on a mountain bike consists of a spring that moves up and down while going over obstacles and a damper that is filled with oil to disperse shock. Together, these parts form the shock absorber.

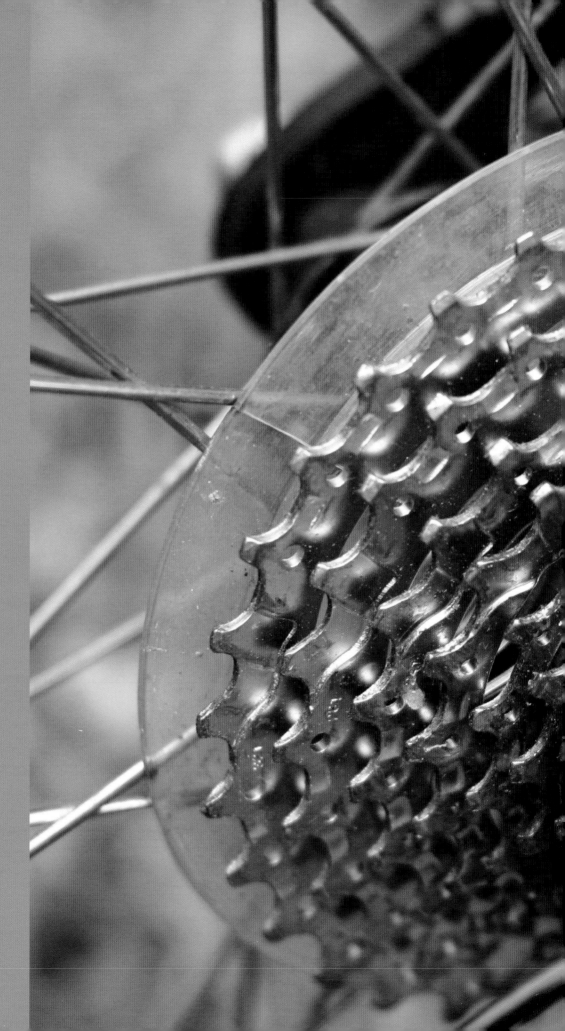

Shifters located on the handlebars control a bike's gears and mechanisms such as the cassette. Pressing the shifter moves a cable that triggers the derailleur, which allows the chain to change gears on the cassette.

to compress when riding over obstacles. Thus, the bike—and not the biker's back—absorbs the impact of bumps. Bikers who do most of their riding on mountain trails often prefer soft tail bikes, which save wear and tear on the body, while those who ride primarily on gravel and paved roads can get by with a hard tail bike. Hard tail bikes are generally $400 to $1,000 cheaper than soft tail bikes, which can cost anywhere from $600 to $2,000.

Mountain bikes are perhaps most recognizable by their fat, knobby tires, but not all mountain bike tires are the same. For all-around trail riding, tires with large knobs to bite into loose surfaces are ideal. Such tires can wear out quickly if ridden extensively on the road, so bikers can outfit their bikes with slick tires—which have relatively little tread—for road riding. For a mix of road and hard-packed trail riding, tires with a relatively smooth bottom tread and additional knobs on the sides for cornering on loose terrain perform well. For those who thrive on the adrenaline rush of a steep downhill pitch, tires designed to deal with high-speed braking are a necessity, as is an aggressive tread pattern.

A bike's smaller components—such as front and rear derailleurs, brakes, cassettes, and chain rings—also influence its price and performance. Low-end derailleurs, for example, can cost as little as $20, while high-end computerized derailleurs can cost $750 or more. Brakes, too, come in a wide variety of styles and prices, from $25 rim brakes to $400 hydraulic disc brakes. Cassettes and chain rings tend to be a bit more consistent in price—generally around $50 to $150—but certain materials, such as carbon, can add significantly to the cost of such components. Bikers today also have a wide range of choices in handlebars, saddles, and pedals, allowing them to choose the system that is most comfortable and efficient for them.

Gearing Up:
Safety and Clothing

While a bike is the most obvious piece of equipment needed for mountain biking, it is certainly not the only thing mountain bikers need. Bikers must also invest in safety equipment, for without it, mountain biking can be a dangerous sport. The helmet is by far the most important piece of safety equipment, protecting the head from smashing against rocks or trees in the event of a fall. Made of strong, durable plastic and available in an assortment of colors, today's helmets can even be a statement in fashion and individuality.

Some helmets include visors to help shield the biker's eyes from the sun. For those who wear helmets without visors, sunglasses are essential, not only to shield the eyes from the sun's rays, but also to protect them from wind, bugs, and dirt. Sunglasses with non-breakable lenses are safest, since there is less risk of shattered glass piercing the eyes in a fall.

Although not the first piece of equipment that comes to mind when thinking about mountain biking safety, gloves are also important. When falling, the hands are usually the first to hit the ground, and gloves—either in half-finger or full-finger styles—provide protection against cuts, scrapes, and "road burn." Gloves also provide comfort while riding, with pads on the palms to limit pressure from gripping the handlebars.

Mountain biking is a great way to experience new terrain. Riding trails can also teach a biker about local history. The Indian Springs Trail in Arizona follows historic railroad routes that cut across the state's rugged landscape.

Mountain biking shorts, also intended to increase comfort, provide extra cushioning for long-distance rides. Although many bikers wear tight Lycra shorts, new shorts are baggier to increase comfort. Mountain biking tights with padding are also available for winter riding.

Mountain bike shoes, specially designed to allow bikers to pedal more efficiently, enable bikers to not only push down, but also pull up on the pedal. The most efficient biking shoes have cleats on the bottom that attach directly to the pedal. Bikers who do not wear cleated shoes have a toe clip component bolted to their pedals. The toe clip fits over a generic biking shoe and holds the foot to the pedal with a tightening strap.

Mountain biking is a high-exertion sport, and hydration is essential, so bikers need to keep a water bottle or hydration system with them at all times. Hydration systems usually consist of a rubber bag, called a bladder, which holds multiple quarts of water. A rubber hose runs out of the bottom of the bladder and has a small mouthpiece on the end. Polyester tubing surrounds the hose to prevent water from freezing in it during cold-weather rides. Hydration systems can often be placed in a backpack, and the hose can be attached to a strap of the backpack near the shoulder, allowing a rider to drink without stopping.

Another essential piece of equipment, the repair kit saves time and frustration in the case of a flat tire or other equipment malfunction. At a minimum, repair kits usually contain a spare tube, a mini-pump, and a small multi-tool. Tire patch kits and levers may also come in handy. All of these items fit inside a small bag, which can be attached under the bike seat. Repair kits can be bought pre-assembled, or bikers can put together their own custom kits.

Invented in 1984, the toe clip allows a biker to pedal efficiently. Road bikes have a clip on one side of the pedal. Mountain bike pedals are the same, although some mountain bikes have clips on both sides of the pedal as well as a wide petal platform, which allow a biker's feet to maneuver freely.

MounJain Biking Techniques

Mountain biking is a sport of balance, skill, and technique. No rider can complete a difficult up- or downhill ride by staying in one gear or stopping at every obstacle. Thus, mountain bikers need to learn several techniques in order to become proficient riders. Because of the danger of injuries, mountain bikers usually practice new techniques and stunts in bike parks or on streets before they attempt them on the trail.

One of the most essential mountain biking skills to master is that of shifting gears. Today's mountain bikes have up to 30 gears, and knowing how to correctly use them helps a rider save valuable energy. Lower gears make pedaling easier and are often used during uphill climbs. Higher gears make it harder to pedal, but since they also slow the rate of pedaling, they often limit exertion when biking across flat terrain. Proficient bikers learn to shift to a lower gear—just before going up a hill—in order to maintain momentum. When little ground is gained despite rapid pedaling, a biker shifts into a higher gear so that the pedaling becomes slower, and more distance is covered with each revolution of the pedals.

Even when a rider has perfected the technique of shifting, some hills may be too steep to climb while seated. By standing on the pedals, bikers can build enough momentum to reach the top. Leaning forward while standing can help to increase balance and efficiency.

Not every mountain bike can handle varying terrain. Bike manufacturers produce

different bike frames, brakes, chains, cassettes, and pedals for specific riding styles.

For example, the Freestyle is a type of bike that is smaller and lighter than most

mountain bikes and is designed for better obstacle avoidance.

Bikers who savor the thrill of speeding downhill can find a challenge in La Paz, Bolivia. The road descending from the world's highest capital is called "The World's Most Dangerous Road" and offers a descent of almost 11,800 feet (3,596 m). The ride begins in the snow-covered Andes Mountains and ends in the Amazon rain forest.

While learning how to bike uphill is important, a huge part of mountain biking involves speeding downhill over bumps and other obstacles. In order to limit the impact these obstacles have on the body, bikers must learn to stand while balancing with the pedals in the 3 o'clock and 9 o'clock positions. Bending the elbows while in this position helps to absorb shock, and leaning the body back so that the seat is between the legs and the body is in line with the rear tire aids in balance.

Extreme mountain bikers don't limit themselves to riding over bumps and hills; they attempt drops off of rocks and mounds, too. Ridden over improperly, drops can impact the body heavily and cause injuries ranging from scrapes and bruises to broken bones and severe lacerations. To properly execute a ride over a drop or mound, a biker needs to stand on the pedals with his or her elbows and knees bent. By keeping the joints loose and malleable, rather than stiffening up, a biker can reduce the likelihood of injury.

Mountain biking can be physically grueling when one is climbing steep inclines. Often, bikers will stand on pedals to increase power, but this method can drain leg energy. An alternative to expending so much energy is to dismount and carry the bike up steep climbs.

More advanced movements, such as the log hop, can help riders get over large rocks or other obstacles on a trail. To perform the log hop, a rider approaches an obstacle at a slow to moderate speed. Just before reaching the obstacle, the rider stands on the pedals and pushes down on the handlebars with his or her body to create spring in the front tire. Quickly pushing the body away from the handlebars causes the front wheel to lift up and over the obstacle. To clear the obstacle with the back wheel, the rider must minimize the weight on the pedals by leaning heavily on the handlebars. The rider can also pop the rear wheel over the obstacle by placing the pedals in the 2 o'clock and 8 o'clock positions, then quickly cranking them to the 12 o'clock and 6 o'clock positions when the rear wheel makes contact with the obstacle.

As a biker improves, he or she can begin to attempt other advanced biking techniques and stunts.

There are always new skills to learn in mountain biking. Many bikers practice complex moves such as track stands, log hops, and wheelies on well-known trails before they attempt putting them to use on unfamiliar terrain.

Being able to perform fundamental mountain biking techniques permits a biker to maneuver over even problem areas on a difficult trail with ease. Being comfortable and confident on the bike allows a biker more freedom to explore the landscape.

One of the best-known mountain biking stunts is the wheelie. To perform a wheelie, a rider remains seated and leans back while lifting the handlebars and front wheel off the ground. By cranking the pedals quickly, the rider can move forward on the rear wheel. To return the front wheel to the ground, the rider simply slows the movements of the pedals and lowers the handlebars.

The bunny hop—another advanced move—lifts both tires off of the ground at the same time. To bunny hop, a biker approaches the object he or she wants to clear at a moderate speed. Standing on the pedals, the biker crouches, bending the knees and elbows as much as possible. Then, the biker springs up, pulling up on the handlebars and the pedals to raise the bike into the air. As with most biking moves, the shock of the landing should be absorbed by bent elbows and knees.

Practicing a new skill or riding a new trail often results in falls for beginners and experts alike. If a biker is wearing biking shoes that clip to the pedals, he or she must know how to disengage them in order to prevent the bike from landing on top of him or her in a fall. With cleated biking shoes, the biker must quickly turn the heel outward and away from the bike, causing the clip to dislodge and free the foot. If a biker is using toe clips, the foot should be pulled straight back out of the tightening strap.

Although it can seem difficult or dangerous at first, learning to bunny hop—or to become airborne off of natural jumps—soon feels natural and becomes a valuable part of any mountain biker's repertoire of skills.

Rating Mountain Biking Trails

From rolling foothills to jagged mountain peaks, almost any terrain holds potential for mountain bikers. Of course, which trail a biker chooses to attempt is not only a matter of preference, but also of skill and experience. Before hitting a trail, bikers must know whether or not they possess the skills necessary to negotiate its terrain. This is not always easy since there is no nationally or internationally recognized mountain bike trail rating system. Fortunately, most of the popular trails in North America have developed rating systems of their own. The National Forest System in the United States, which boasts more than 130,000 miles (209,200 km) of trails, has adopted a three-tier, color-coded system to describe the level of difficulty of its trails.

Trails marked with a green circle cover the mildest terrain—with gentle slopes and few obstacles—and are appropriate for anyone, even novices. These trails are well marked and easy to follow. Blue square markings on trail signs signify trails that are more difficult. Intermediate through advanced users should be comfortable on these trails and can expect to encounter at least some obstacles, such as rocks, boulders, and logs, along the way. Blue trails are often moderately steep and narrow, requiring bikers to exercise caution.

Mountain biking is generally done at a much slower pace—usually 20 miles (32 km) or fewer per hour—than road biking. Biking speed depends in part on how steep or rugged the trail is, and in part on how brave the rider is.

New challenges always await avid mountain bikers. One memorable challenge is riding the Great Divide Mountain Bike Route. This trail is 2,490 miles (4,007 km) of off-road terrain that runs from Canada to Mexico, following and crossing the Continental Divide.

Trails marked with a black box are labeled "most difficult." These trails are recommended for advanced and expert riders only, since the terrain is certain to be steep, and trails may not be well marked. Black trails are often littered with obstacles, some of which may be difficult to see. Individuals using these trails must be able to navigate using a map and compass or a **Global Positioning System (GPS).** Survival skills in the case of an accident or emergency are essential, since these trails may take riders high up a mountainside or into wilderness areas that are far from help.

While many State Park Systems around the U.S. have adopted the forest system's trail ratings, some states, such as Texas and California, have created their own systems. Most private biking clubs have also created their own standards for rating specific trails. Although most trail rating systems are similar, bikers should always research the rating system utilized in an area before taking off down the trail.

Hit The Trail

Today, millions of mountain biking trails line the globe, each with its own unique characteristics: following a river, meandering around jagged, desolate peaks, sporting a thick covering of hardwood or rain forest, winding across endless open desert. Whatever the main attraction of a trail, exploring it from the back of a bike gives riders a unique opportunity to explore the land. As American author Ernest Hemingway put it: "It is by riding a bicycle that you learn the contours of a country best, since you have to sweat up the hills and coast down them."

The Black Hills of South Dakota provide plenty of hills for bikers to sweat up and down. This national forest offers 1.2 million acres (485,625 ha) of ponderosa pine forests, open grasslands, and rugged rock formations, criss-crossed by more than 400 miles (645 km) of trails open to mountain bikers. The area's Centennial Route, a trail for experienced riders, winds through 111 miles (179 km) of the most heavily forested backcountry in the Black Hills and leads riders through Wind Cave National Park, Mount Rushmore National Park, and Bear Butte State Park. Another extensive trail, the 114-mile (183 km) Mickelson Trail, provides gentle slopes suitable for all riders. This exceptional trail crosses more than 100 converted railroad bridges and passes through 4 rock tunnels.

For riders who can handle a steep climb, the trail offers amazing views of Hell Canyon's wildflowers and pine trees. Bikers in the Black Hills are often rewarded with stunning views not only of the land, but also of wildlife, including white-tailed deer, mule deer, elk, grouse, and turkeys, as well as the occasional mountain lion.

The Kettle Moraine State Forest in southern Wisconsin also offers incredible terrain for bikers of all levels, with more than 100 miles (161 km) of trails. The unique John Muir trail provides five different loops to accommodate everyone from the beginner to the advanced rider. The easiest loop travels 1.5 miles (2.4 km) through open fields and scattered pines and hardwoods, while the most difficult trail covers 10 miles (16 km) of steep, rocky hills and old-growth forest. The Emma Carlin trail also offers a selection of difficulty levels, and the five-mile (8 km) Connector trail, which runs between the John Muir and Emma Carlin trails, leads bikers over some of the roughest terrain in the Kettle Moraine.

As both sport and recreation, mountain biking continues to grow in popularity around the world. In countries such as Ecuador, where tourism is big business, people can rent mountain bikes and arrange to take bike tours.

In the spring of 2005, the
International Mountain
Biking Association (IMBA)
and the National Park
System (NPS) reached
an agreement to allow
mountain bikers access to
hundreds of dirt roads that
were previously closed to
bikes. In return, the IMBA
will help the NPS create
more off-road bike trails.

The White Mountains National Forest of New Hampshire is another popular mountain biking destination. Here, an extensive network of trails runs through woodlands and winds around spectacular ridgelines. The 25-mile-long (40 km) Cherry Mountain Loop climbs more than 1,500 feet (457 m) and offers views of three beautiful waterfalls. Several area ski resorts also play host to mountain bikers every summer, offering everything from packed gravel cross-country trails to downhill terrain reached by ski lift.

For those looking to hone their technical biking skills, Whistler Mountain Bike Park, situated in the Coast Mountains near Vancouver, Canada, offers more than 125 miles (200 km) of trails. Featuring jumps, drop-offs, **tabletops**, **berms**, and more, trails here can challenge even the most experienced riders, although the park also offers several beginner-level trails. Considered by many to be the number-one bike park in the world, Whistler also offers skill centers designed to help beginning, intermediate, and advanced riders perfect their technique, as well as a dirt jump course created by John Cowan, one of the best dirt jumpers in the world. For the most daring expert riders, the park's Garbanzo Zone provides steep, ski lift accessed hills, with descents of up to 2,165 vertical feet (660 m).

Olympic competitors in cross-country cycling train year-round. Altitude training in mountains, weightlifting, and constant bike riding all help to prepare elite bikers' bodies and skills for competition.

Competitions and Festivals

Mountain biking requires a unique combination of balance and endurance, concentration and guts. With competitions in categories ranging from the traditional cross-country race to the extreme obstacle course, this adventure sport offers heart-stopping thrills to competitors and fans alike.

Cross-country mountain biking made its debut at the 1996 Summer Olympics in Atlanta, Georgia, and remains the only mountain biking discipline recognized as an Olympic sport. At the 2004 Olympics in Athens, Greece, the mountain biking course traveled up Mount Parnitha, a 4,635-foot (1,413 m) peak, and challenged competitors with narrow, rocky descents and exposed ascents. In the men's event, Julien Absalon of France averaged 12 miles (19 km) per hour over the 26.9-mile (43.3 km) race, completing it in 2 hours and 15 minutes to take the gold. Although no North America men medaled in the 2004 Olympics, Seamus McGrath of Canada placed 9th, and American Todd Wells placed 19th in a field of 50 competitors.

In the women's competition, which covered 19.4 miles (31.3 km), Norwegian Gunn-Rita Dahle took the gold, averaging 10 miles (16 km) per hour for a time of just over 1 hour, 56 minutes. North Americans had a much stronger showing in the women's competition, with Canadians Marie-Helene Premont and Alison Sydor placing second and fourth respectively. Mary McConneloug from the U.S. also performed well, placing ninth.

Although the Olympics is the most elite event for cross-country mountain bikers, there are plenty of other opportunities for avid bikers to compete. The annual International Cycling Union (UCI) Mountain Biking World Championships is second only to the Olympics in importance for cross-country racers and is the most elite event for racers in the team relay, downhill, four-cross, and trials disciplines.

In the men's cross-country race at the 2004 World Championships, held in Les Gets, France, Olympic gold-medalist Julien Absalon rode his way to gold on a gold bike with a gold saddle, wearing a gold helmet. Absalon finished the muddy 23.4-mile (37.7 km) race with a time of 2 hours, 20 minutes. In the women's race also, the 2004 Olympic gold-medalist was crowned world champion, as Gunn-Rita Dahle completed the 19.5-mile (31.4 km) race in 2 hours and 2 minutes.

Another cross-country discipline in the World Championships is the team relay, in which one elite male rider, one elite female rider, one male rider younger than 23, and one junior rider from each country race as a team. At the 2004 World Championships, each team member completed one lap of the 3.9-mile (6.3 km) course, and the Canadian team raced to a stunning victory, beating second-place Switzerland by 24 seconds.

One of the most thrilling World Championship events, the downhill, requires bikers to plunge one at a time down a steep hill covered with jumps, bumps, corners, and drop-offs. The rider with the fastest time wins the event. Fabien Barel of France beat out 105 racers at the 2004 World Championships to take the gold, flying down the 1.3-mile (2.1 km) course at an average speed of 29.2 miles (47 km) per hour to finish in 2 minutes, 40 seconds. Vanessa Quin of New Zealand averaged 24.9 miles (40.1 km) per hour to win the women's event with a time of 3 minutes, 8 seconds.

Competitors in the four-cross discipline—added to the World Championships in 2002—ride four at a time on a short track (usually about 820 feet, or 250 m, long) with sharp turns and several jumps.

Mountain biking competitions are not limited to riding trails or courses. Some extreme mountain biking competitions have bikers compete on obstacle courses in which stunts such as back flips and aerial tricks are attempted and scored by a panel of judges.

The event involves a series of elimination rounds until only four competitors remain to race in the final round. Eric Carter of the U.S. and Jana Horakova of the Czech Republic raced to gold at the 2004 World Championships.

The final World Championship event, the trials competition, requires advanced riding and numerous stunts as riders negotiate a course strewn with obstacles such as logs and concrete blocks. The riders' goal is to clear the obstacles without allowing any body part to touch the ground. Riders receive a penalty point every time they touch the ground, and the rider with the fewest penalties wins. The men's trials competition is divided into two categories—one for those riding bikes with 20-inch (50.8 cm) wheels, and one for 26-inch (66 cm) wheels. Benito Ros Charral of Spain took the world championship title in the 20-inch (50.8 cm) category in 2004, while his countryman Daniel Comas Riera won the 26-inch (66 cm) event. In the women's competition—which includes only 26-inch (66 cm) wheels—Karin Moor of Switzerland was victorious.

Of course, most people ride mountain bikes for recreation rather than competition. Mountain bike festivals across North America cater to both competitive and non-competitive bikers every year. CrankWorx, formerly known as the Whistler Mountain Bike Festival, takes place annually at Whistler Mountain Bike Park. The five-day festival offers competitions, outdoor expositions, professional riding demonstrations, music, and entertainment.

The third-oldest annual mountain bike festival in the world, Rage in the Sage, takes place in the Gunnison-Crested Butte area of Colorado every May. This festival often hosts up to 300 racers, who ride over high-desert terrain in cross-country, road, and 50-mile (80.5 km) marathon races.

Colorado also hosts the oldest mountain bike festival, Fat Tire Bike Week, every June. This five-day event celebrated its 25th anniversary in 2005. The more than 300 bikers at this festival can attend biking clinics and join bike

While some bike competitions may last only for an afternoon, the annual 24-Hour National Mountain Biking Championship gives bikers a chance to race around the clock on difficult, wooded trails in Wausau, Wisconsin's, Nine Mile County Forest.

tours led by local riders. To add to the fun, many participants wear costumes, take part in a mountain bike rodeo, and display tricks while riding through downtown streets.

The Sea Otter Classic, held in April at the Laguna Seca Recreational Area in Monterey, California, serves both mountain and road bikers. Attracting more than 45,000 biking fans, this 4-day festival features races in more than 226 categories, including downhill, dirt jumping, and cross-country. With races for beginners, juniors, experts, and seniors, there are plenty of opportunities for everyone to get involved. During the event, bikers can explore the displays of more than 250 vendors eager to demonstrate the latest biking technology and equipment.

With so many competitions, festivals, and fans, it's no wonder that mountain biking is one of the most popular adventure sports in the world. Today, four out of every five bikes sold in countries such as the U.S., Britain, Canada, Australia, and New Zealand are mountain bikes, and as equipment continues to advance, the sport is only likely to grow more popular. New frame materials, such as magnesium, hold the potential to make bikes stronger and better than ever. Advanced clothing materials also hold the promise of increased comfort during long-distance rides, making the sport even more appealing to people worldwide. As more and more people hit the trails, they will discover what mountain bikers around the world have known for three decades: nothing compares to the thrill of the ride.

Mountain biking is an exceptional way to strengthen and tone the body, learn new and useful skills, join other athletes in competitions, and experience the beauty of nature. Every day, more people come to appreciate and participate in this accessible adventure sport.

RECOMMENDED READING

Crowther, Nicky. *The Ultimate Mountain Bike Book: The Definitive Illustrated Guide to Bikes, Components, Techniques, Thrills, and Trails.* Buffalo, N.Y.: Firefly Books, 2002.

Mountain Bike Magazine. *Mountain Bike Magazine's Complete Guide to Mountain Biking Skills: Expert Tips on Conquering Curves, Dips, Descents, Hills, Water Hazards, and All Other Terrain Hazards.* New York: St. Martin's Press, 1996.

Richards, Brant, and Steve Worland. *The Complete Book of Mountain Biking.* London: Harper Collins, 1997.

Roll, Bob. *Bobke II.* Boulder, Colo.: VeloPress, 2003.

Strassman, Michael. *Basic Essentials of Mountain Biking.* Guilford, Conn.: Globe Pequot Press, 2000.

WEB SITES OF INTEREST

www.americantrails.org
Provides details about trails located across the U.S., as well as current news and events and a member posting board.

www.bikewebsite.com
Offers advice on how to repair, maintain, and purchase bikes.

www.crankworx.com
Provides information on the CrankWorx bike festival.

www.norbanationals.com
Offers information on races sponsored by the National Off-Road Biking Association (NORBA) across the U.S.

www.mbaction.com
Provides photos, descriptions of equipment, tips, and current events in the mountain biking arena.

www.mountainbike.com
Home page of *Mountain Bike* magazine, featuring information on bikes, gear, and riding locations.

www.pedalinghistory.com
Provides a look into the history of bicycles and their transformation over time.

www.trailsource.com
Aids in locating trails worldwide for mountain biking, dirt biking, hiking, and more.

www.usacycling.org
Home of USA cycling, the organization that selects cyclists to represent the U.S. in international competitions.

www.webmountainbike.com
Provides links, stories, pictures, tips, troubleshooting, and quotes about mountain biking.

ww1.whistlerblackcomb.com/bike
Provides information about Whistler Mountain Bike Park, and its various camps, tours, and events.

GLOSSARY

aluminum alloy—a metal consisting of a combination of aluminum and another metal or two forms of aluminum

balloon-tire bikes—bikes made in the 1930s–50s; they featured wide, low-pressure tires, a streamlined frame, one gear, and brakes operated by pedaling backward

berms—built-up, banked turns

cassettes—five to eight gears located on the rear of the bike

chain rings—rings that rotate to move the bike forward; the chain ring is located near the pedals and typically consists of two or three big gears

components—devices that allow riders to pedal, shift, brake, and turn the bike; everything that is on the bike other than the frame

cyclo-cross—an off-road bike race that requires riders to dismount and run with their bikes over obstacles

derailleurs—devices that allow the shifting of gears by moving the bike chain to and from different-sized sprocket wheels

disc brakes—brakes that press against a disc on the hub of the wheel

drum brakes—brakes that press against the inside of a cylindrical drum attached to the wheel hub

epoxy resin—a tough, synthetic resin (semi-solid substance) that sets up after heat or pressure is applied; used for adhesives, coatings, and laminates

front fork—the location on the front of the bike where the frame divides into two sections that attach to either side of the wheel

Global Positioning System (GPS)—a navigational system involving satellites and computers; it is used to determine the latitude and longitude of a receiver on Earth

multi-tool—a compact device that contains many tools; usually, the tools are pulled out of the device individually and locked into place

rim brakes—brakes that squeeze the rim of the wheel

suspension systems—series of shock absorbers located on the front and back of a bike to decrease the impact of bumps and jolts on a rider's body

tabletops—jumps with a ramp on either side of a long, flat top

INDEX